THE JOURNEY WITHIN

Poems to Navigate the Journey of Life.

ARNAB SARMA

BookLeaf
Publishing

India | USA | UK

This book is dedicated to all those people who are facing difficult transitions, seeking motivation to overcome life's obstacles or simply looking to find deeper meaning in their everyday experiences.

As we navigate the winding path of our lives, it's easy to become consumed by the day-to-day challenges and lose sight of the bigger picture.

Therefore, in this powerful collection of poems, I invite you all to embark on a journey of self-discovery and illuminate your life path forward.

Acknowledgement

I want to thank all those people who helped me directly or indirectly and knowingly or unknowingly in understanding the true meaning of life. Their support has made me a better person, allowing me to know my true self and also to understand the true face of others.

Lastly, I want to thank my father (Prof) Dr. Jogendra Nath Sarma, my mother Anjalee Sarma, my elder sister Atabi Sarma, my brother-in-law Trinayan Dev Sharma, my niece Adriti Bharadwaj, my wife Lucky Gogoi and my daughter Akanshya Bharadwaj.

Preface

The journey of life is rarely a straight and smooth path. It is filled with twists and turns, highs and lows, joys and sorrows. Yet, it is through navigating these varied experiences that we find the true essence of what it means to be human.

In this powerful collection of poems, you will embark on a reflective exploration of the lessons that can be gleaned from life's journey.

Let the words in the poems be the beacon that illuminates the lessons to be learned, the beauty to be savored and the inspiration to keep moving forward, no matter what challenges arise. For in the end, it is the journey itself that gives life its profound meaning and beauty.

Overcome

There will be people to hurt you,
Spend more time with those who love you.
You may have regrets,
Unless you can get time back.

Focus on your happiness,
Pour your love on people who need it.
Obstacles are challenges to sharpen the mind,
Every fear you overcome will make you shine.

Happiness

Happiness must not come,
From what lies outside of you.
See the happiness from within,
How you perceive life from inside.

Keep the tendency to focus on positive
experiences,
And treasure them for frequent recall.
Dim all memories of distressing times,
That's the major key to a happy life.

Time

Life is complicated,
Problems will come to us.
Stress is the distraction,
From what's really important to us.

Don't wait for things to get better,
Count on the things that matter.
Learn to be happy right now,
Otherwise, time will run out forever.

Move On

Sometimes, let people go,
To preserve your sanity,
To guard your health,
And to protect your heart.

Sometimes, those people are,
The family members,
As they know very well,
The buttons that push you back.

Sometimes, you have to release,
And move on from such people.
Sometimes, you have to forget,
And move on so that they regret.

Peace Amidst Chaos

Treat past as a brilliant teacher,
And the future as a beckoning light.
Feel the presence of the wave now,
Reveling in the cool, wet sparkle of nature.

In the midst of all the chaos,
Shed away confusion and pressure.
Create and inhabit for yourself,
To rest in the peaceful lap of nature.

Takes Time

Things will take time,
The efforts you are making today,
The task you are doing today,
Will rarely produce instant results.
Be patient.
Watch and make all the adjustments,
Try to polish your plan.
The seeds you will plant today,
Will bud and bloom in the same way.
Will give you more results,
Than you wished for and prayed.

Optimistic Tomorrow

It's time to sleep,
To rest, restore, and rejuvenate.
But you are not able to do so,
You are only looking forward to *doing* it.

You rest your head on the soft pillow,
You snuggle into the blanket.
Feel the blessed peace and escape from the
chaos,
You slowly let everything go.

Your thoughts tuned by choice,
To all your happy memories,
And then you fall asleep,
Feeling all your optimistic tomorrows.

That's Life

A world full of corrupt and evil-doers,
Blinds us to the decent people.
We fail to recognize loyal and trusted people,
And fall prey to the evil strangers.

In a world full of immorality,
It can make you forget all the rewards,
To cling to what is right.

In a world full of nastiness,
It can block your awareness,
Of all the things good in your life.

Keep yourself protected against the bad,
Try to embrace and enjoy the good,
And that's called life.

Mistake

Mistake is a valuable teacher,
With a lesson to learn forever.
Write this new knowledge down,
And apply it to make your life better.

When you make a mistake,
Just ask yourself, what do you earn from this?
With a beautiful mistake you made,
Learning from it just made your life great.

Live Your Life

Stop trying to get from people,
What they cannot or will not give.
To ease your stress,
Just focus on yourself.

You can flee from them,
Or you can choose to accept them.
Live your life the way you want,
As much as you can.

Live In The Moment

Gently look at your past,
And enjoy the pleasant memories.
Learn from your past,
So you don't repeat mistakes again.

Live in the moment,
Stop to see, hear, and feel.
Wallow in the sensual pleasure of the present,
Take time to escape the past and the future.

You Are In Control

Rein in the past,
When it creates sadness or anger,
You are in control,
What you choose to think and feel.

Never let the past,
Withdraw energy from the present.
Peace is not needing to know,
Everything that will happen.

Focus

Sometimes life hands us burdens,
The burdens which we can't change.
We try anyway with all our energy,
But only experience pain with no gain.

Accept the things you can't change,
And focus on something that truly means.
Take the energy and time you are wasting,
Focus on the pleasure of creating something.

Today

Take your life one day at a time,
To enjoy what is to be enjoyed today.
The past cannot be changed,
Fill your life with new pleasure today.

Stop worrying about the future,
The things that may or may not happen.
See the exciting possibilities of today,
And say, *I will make the most of today.*

Love Yourself

The years will pass in the blink of an eye,
Moments of sadness and joy will all fly by.
People you love will come and disappear,
The world will not stop for you to suffer.

All the worries and fears,
That plagued you each day.
In the end of it all,
Will just fade away.

It's really important how much kindness,
And love you show to yourself.
Before the Lord tells you,
It's your time to go.

Moment

Don't let your mind wander,
To what's coming next.
Cherish this moment,
And give it your best.

It can take a moment,
To change your life's path.
And once it ticks by,
There is no going back.

Up to You

You become who you are,
In those moments you live.
And the growth's not in taking,
But in how much you give.

Life is just moments,
So precious and few.
Whether valued or squandered,
It's all up to you.

It's Only

It's only when we close our eyes,
Our dreams seem to be clear and bright.
It's only in our darkest time,
We truly see the light.

It's only when we lose our way,
We pray to the God above.
It's only in the time of grief,
We seek the true meaning of love.

Mark on the Earth

You must be proud of who you've tried to be,
And this life you chose to live.
Make the most of every day,
By giving all you have to give.

Stand up with courage,
Despite standing on your own.
Still get up and face each day,
Even when you feel alone.

Live a life that matters,
To be someone of great worth.
To love and be loved in return,
And make your mark on the Earth.

Journey

It is all about the journey,
And what has yet to come.
Life is what you make of it,
You are what you've become.

Life is too short,
To hold onto regrets.
Forgiveness is the key,
Though you may never forget.

Cherish the good,
And remove the bad.
Some people don't realize,
Till it's gone what they've had.

Moving on is a way of life,
There will always be obstacles, pain and strife.

Golden Proposal

You must believe that you are strong enough
to fight,
You have to believe in yourself to do what is
right.
Always do for YOU no matter what you do,
In the end, the only one who has your back is
you.

Your chance to live is now,
So what are you waiting for?
The world is yours for the taking,
And so much more.

Endless possibilities are forever at your
disposal,
The chance to live another day,
Is life's golden proposal.

www.ingramcontent.com/pod-product-compliance
Lightning Source LLC
Chambersburg PA
CBHW071247140726
47996CB00007B/2790

Through the lyrical verse of the poems, it will remind you that even in our darkest moments, there is light to be found. Whether you are facing difficult transition, seeking motivation to overcome an obstacle or simply looking to find deeper meaning in your everyday experiences, this collection of poems will undoubtly leave an indelible mark to navigate the winding path of your own life's journey.

ABOUT THE AUTHOR

Mr Arnab Sarma was born and brought up in Dibrugarh of the North-Eastern part of Indian state Assam. He grew passion for writing and is inspired by his father who is also an author. Mr Arnab, being inclined towards poetry began writing poems from an early age and had published it in various newspapers and magazines.

Besides his interest in poetry, Mr Arnab Sarma is a journalist by profession and a photographer. He has also won various awards through his photography.

EMILY WOOSLEY

MEDITATE